101 Life Skills Every Kid Needs to Know

101 Life Skills Every Kid Needs to Know

Matilda Walsh

Books by Matilda Walsh

101 Life Skills Every Kid Needs to Know

101 Life Skills and Tips for Teens

Adulting for Beginners

Table of Contents

Introduction

Hello, young adventurers! Welcome to the world of life skills. In this book, you'll learn all sorts of awesome tricks and tips that will help you become a superstar in life. You'll learn how to make friends, do well in tests, cook simple meals, be kind to the environment, grow vegetables, make smart decisions and set goals.

Now, you might be thinking, "What are life skills anyway?" Well, life skills are like superpowers that you can use to make your life easier and more fun. They're things like how to talk to people, manage your time, and deal with stress. And the best part is, everyone can learn them!

In this book, we'll take you on a journey through the world of life skills. You'll learn how to be brave, solve problems, and even start a business. This book has lots of fun ways to teach you important life skills like talking to people, fixing problems, making decisions, and many more. These skills will help you go through life and be ready for anything with confidence and a positive attitude. So, whether you want to make new friends, deal with hard things, or just be the best you can be, this book can help you. You're about to become a superhero and start an exciting journey to take control of your life. Are you ready? Let's do it!

How to be successful in school

School helps you learn many things that will help you in your life. You can learn how to read, write, and do math, which are all important skills to have. You can also learn about science, history, and many other subjects that can help you understand the world around you. School can also help you make friends and learn how to work with others. When you go to school, you can grow up to be whatever you want to be, like a doctor, a teacher, a business owner or a scientist. Everything is possible! Here are some handy tips to have fun and succeed in school.

Listen to your teacher and follow their instructions.

Your teacher is there to help you learn and grow, and they want you to do your best. When your teacher talks, try to listen carefully and pay attention to what they're saying. If they give you instructions or tell you what to do, make sure you follow them as best you can. This will help you learn and also show your teacher that you're responsible and respectful. If you have trouble understanding something, don't be afraid to ask your teacher for help. They are there to support you and want you to succeed. So always try your best to listen to your teacher and follow their instructions, and you'll do great in school!

Always do your homework and turn it in on time.

Doing your homework helps you practice what you learned in class and get better at it. When you get your homework, make sure to read the instructions carefully and ask your teacher if you have any questions. Then, find a quiet place to work and do your best. Try to finish your homework before it's due, so you don't have to rush and can check it over for mistakes. When you're done, make sure to put your name on it and turn it in to your teacher on time. This shows your teacher that you're responsible and that you care about your schoolwork. If you need help, be sure to ask your parents or a kind adult for help.

Study for tests and quizzes, and ask for help if you need it.

Tests and quizzes are important ways for your teacher to see how well you understand what you've been learning in class. It's a good idea to study for them so you can do your best. When you have a test or quiz coming up, make sure to study a little bit each day. You can go over your notes or ask your teacher for a study guide. It's also helpful to find a quiet place to work and to take breaks when you need to. If you have trouble understanding something, don't be afraid to ask your teacher or a classmate for help. They can find a way to explain it so makes sense. Asking for help is a smart thing to do, and it can help you do better on your test or quiz.

Be kind to your classmates and work together when you can.

When you're kind to others, you can make friends and feel happier in school. It's important to work together with your classmates too, because sometimes you can accomplish more as a team than you can alone. When you work together, you can share ideas and learn from each other. Remember, school is more fun when you have friends, and working together is a great way to make new ones!

Take breaks when you need to, and get plenty of rest at night.

Taking breaks and getting enough rest is important for your health and for doing well in school. When you're studying or working on a project, it's okay to take a break if you start to feel tired or frustrated. You can stretch, take a walk, or do something fun for a little while. Taking a break can help you feel refreshed and ready to keep going. It's also important to get plenty of rest at night. Your body and brain need sleep to recharge, so try to go to bed at the same time every night and get at least 8 hours of sleep. When you're well-rested, you'll feel better and be able to focus better in school.

Ask questions if you don't understand.

It's okay to ask questions in school if you don't understand something. Asking questions can help you learn and can also help other kids who might have the same question. If you're confused about something, raise your hand and ask your teacher. They will be happy to explain it to you in a way that makes sense. If you're too shy to ask in front of the whole class, you can ask your teacher after class or during a break. It's important to remember that everyone learns differently, and it's okay if you need a little extra help. So, don't be afraid to ask questions if you're unsure about something. Your teacher is there to help you! So don't be afraid to ask questions.

Believe in yourself and try your best every day! Remember, going to school can be fun and rewarding if you put in the effort and stay positive.

Being a great friend

Making friends and having strong friendships is really important. It's really nice to have people in your life that you can trust and depend on.

In this book, I'll teach you how to make friends in school and outside of school. You'll learn how to be yourself, be friendly, and make friends quickly. I'll show you how to find common interests and be a reliable friend. Making friends and building relationships can be a fun and exciting journey. Let's get started!

Be yourself

Don't pretend to be someone else, just to try to impress others. Being yourself is the best way to make new friends who will like you because of who you are.

Smile and be friendly

If you smile, this can go a long way in making new friends. It shows that you're approachable and open to meeting new people.

Listen actively

When talking to someone, make sure you actively listen to what they're saying. It shows that you're interested in what they have to say!

Show empathy

Empathy is when you are able to understand and share the feelings of others. It's an important skill to have when building relationships. Put yourself in other people's shoes and understand where they're coming from.

Find common interests

Finding interests you both love is a great way to connect with others. It gives you something to talk about and a reason to spend time together.

Be kind and respectful

Kindness and respect go a long way in making friends. Treat others how you want to be treated to show them that you care.

Making friends in school

Starting a new school year or joining a new school can be exciting, but it can also be a little bit scary. One of the best things about school is making new friends! But how do you make friends in school? Making friends in school can be fun, and it's an essential part of a happy school life. I'll help you feel confident about making new friends. So, are you ready to make new friends? Let's get started!

Smile and say "hello"

A simple smile and a friendly "hello" can go a long way in making new friends. It shows that you're friendly and open to meeting new people.

Join clubs or teams

Joining a club or team is a great way to meet new people who love doing what you do. It's a fun way to make new friends.

Participate in class

Participating in class can help you connect with your classmates and show them that you're interested in learning and making new friends.

Ask questions

Asking questions is really good! This starts people talking and you can get to know someone a lot better. It shows that you're interested in what they have to say.

Be a good listener

It's really good to listen to your friends when they talk. This tells them that you care about what they say and think.

Invite someone to play or eat lunch with you

If you see someone sitting alone or looking bored, invite them to join you for lunch or to play a game. It's a fun way to make people feel less lonely, make new friends and be kind.

Remember, making friends takes time and effort, but it's worth it. Don't be shy to say "hello" and ask your classmates to play with you. Always be a good listener and be helpful when someone needs it. The more you smile, laugh, and enjoy time with others, the more friends you'll make. And always remember, being yourself is the best way to find true friends who like you for who you are. Keep these tips in mind, and you'll make lots of great friends at school!

How to treat your friends

Having friends is really important. Friends can make us happy, help us when we need it, and like the same things we do. But being a good friend means more than just having fun. It means being nice and respectful to your friends. Being kind and respectful to your friends makes your friendships stronger and more special. Do you want to learn how to be an awesome friend? Let's start!

Be kind

Being kind is an amazing thing that you can do for your friends. Say nice things, share your toys or snacks, and be helpful when they need it.

Listen

Listening to your friends is very important. When your friend is talking, listen carefully and show that you care about their opinions and thoughts.

Be respectful

Being kind to your friends is very important. Always be respectful of your friends' feelings, thoughts, and things they have.

Be trustworthy

Trust is critical in any friendship. Keep your promises, be honest, and keep your friend's secrets safe.

Say sorry when you make a mistake

Everyone makes mistakes, but we need to take responsibility for them. If you do something wrong, don't be afraid to say sorry.

Have fun

Friendship is all about having fun together! Play games, laugh, and enjoy spending time together.

Treating your friends with kindness and respect is a two-way street. If you treat your friends well, they are more likely to treat you well in return.

Fixing disagreements with friends

Sometimes friends don't agree with each other, and that's okay. But it's essential to know how to resolve these disagreements so that you and your friend can still be friends.

This book will teach you simple ways to solve problems with your friends. You can learn how to work things out with your friends and have stronger friendships. So, are you ready to learn how to resolve disagreements with your friends? Let's get started!

Talk nicely

Use kind words when you're talking to your friend, even if you're upset.

Listen to each other

Take turns talking and really listen to what your friend is saying.

Find a way to make things better

Work together and see if you can find an answer that makes everyone happy.

Say sorry when you're wrong

If you made a mistake, say sorry and try to make it right.

Forgive each other

If your friend says sorry, try to forgive them.

Take a break if needed

If you're feeling upset or angry, take a break and come back to the conversation later.

Stay calm

Try to stay calm and not raise your voice.

Be respectful

Always be kind and thoughtful when talking to your friend if they have a different opinion, even if you disagree with them.

Ask for help

If you're having trouble resolving the disagreement, ask a trusted adult for help.

Remember, it's important to talk things out with your friends and find a way to work through disagreements. With these tips, you can learn how to resolve disagreements with your friends and have stronger, healthier friendships.

Dealing with peer pressure

Dealing with peer pressure can be tough, especially for kids. Peer pressure happens when someone tries to pressure you into doing something that you don't want to do or is not good for you, just because everyone else is doing it.

It's important to know that you always have a choice and that you don't have to do something just because your friends or peers are doing it. Saying "no" is okay and it's important to stand up for yourself and what you believe in.

Remember that true friends will respect your choices and won't pressure you into doing something that you don't want to do. If you ever feel uncomfortable or unsure, it's always okay to talk to a trusted adult, like a parent, teacher, or counselor, for support and guidance.

How to deal with peer pressure:

Say "no" politely but firmly.

It's okay to say no and stick to what you believe in.

Offer an alternative activity.

If your friends want to do something you don't feel comfortable with, suggest a different activity that you all can enjoy.

Find friends who share your values.

It's important to be friends with people who respect your choices and values.

Be confident in yourself.

Remember there is only one you! And you are perfect exactly as you are. It's okay to be different from your friends.

Talk to a trusted adult.

If you ever feel uncomfortable or unsure about a situation, talk to a trusted adult, like a parent, teacher, or counselor, for support and guidance.

Be a leader, not a follower.

Don't just follow what your friends are doing, be a leader and make your own choices based on what you believe in.

Remember, it's okay to be yourself and make your own decisions. Always trust your instincts and don't let anyone pressure you or force you into doing things you don't want to do.

Setting boundaries & saying no

Sometimes does your life feel out of control? Do you sometimes say yes to things you don't really want to do, just because you don't want to upset someone? It's okay, because we've all been there. But here's the thing: you have the power to set boundaries. You can absolutely say no to things that make you uncomfortable. It's important to have boundaries to protect yourself and your feelings.

Boundaries are like invisible lines that help us feel safe, comfortable, and happy. It's okay to let people know when something doesn't feel right to you or when you need your own space. Boundaries help keep you safe. If a person asks you to do something that feels wrong or unsafe, saying "no" protects you. It's okay to have your own space and time to relax. If you're feeling tired or overwhelmed, setting boundaries helps you feel more comfortable and happy.

Your feelings matter! If something makes you sad or scared, it's important to speak up and say "no." This helps others understand and respect your feelings. When you set boundaries and say "no," you show that you know what's best for you. This helps you feel strong, brave, and in control of your own life.

Remember, it's always okay to set boundaries and say "no" when you need to. This helps you feel safe, happy, and confident, and it helps others understand and respect your feelings, too.

Don't be afraid to stand up for yourself, because you're important!

How to set boundaries

I want to share with you some easy and fun ways to set boundaries and say no when you need to. It's really useful for everyone to learn how to communicate your feelings, assert yourself, and stand up for what you believe in. Remember, setting boundaries and saying no is all about taking care of yourself and being true to who you are. Let's get started!

Know your limits

It's important to understand what makes you uncomfortable or unhappy. Once you know your limits, you can set boundaries to protect yourself.

Say "no" confidently

When you say no, say it confidently and clearly. Don't feel bad about it - you have the right to say no to things that make you uncomfortable.

Use "I" statements

Instead of blaming others, use "I" statements to express how you feel. For example, "I don't feel comfortable doing that" instead of "You're making me uncomfortable."

Be assertive

Assertiveness means standing up for yourself and your boundaries. Practice being assertive by speaking up and expressing yourself confidently.

Don't apologize for saying no

Saying no is not something you should feel sorry for. It's important to stand by your decision and not apologize for it.

Take time to think

If you're not sure about something, take time to think about it before saying yes or no. This can help you make a decision that's right for you.

Surround yourself with supportive people

Having supportive friends and family members can help you feel more confident in setting boundaries and saying no.

Celebrate your successes

When you set boundaries and say no, celebrate your success! It really takes a lot of courage to stand up for yourself and it's important to acknowledge your accomplishments.

Dealing with bullies

Sometimes, kids might bully other kids, and it's not a nice thing to do. There can be different reasons why kids bully. Here are a few:

Feelings

A kid who bullies might be feeling sad, angry, or upset, and they don't know how to handle these feelings properly. So, they might take it out on other kids.

Attention

Sometimes, kids bully because they want attention from others. They might think that being mean will make them more popular or get them noticed.

Learned behavior

If a kid sees others being mean or if they are treated badly at home, they might think that it's okay to act that way with other kids, too.

Differences

Some kids bully others because they don't understand or are not used to differences in people, like how someone looks or what they like to do.

It's important to remember that bullying is never okay, and it's not your fault if someone bullies you. If you see someone being bullied or if you're being bullied, always tell a grown-up, like a parent or teacher, so they can help make things better. Let's work together to make sure everyone feels safe, respected, and happy!

How to deal with bullies

Dealing with bullies can be a scary experience. But it's important to know that you have the power to protect yourself and stand up for yourself. Remember, it's never your fault if someone is bullying you, and you have the right to feel safe and respected.

Here are some ways to deal with bullies:

Stay calm

It's essential to stay calm when dealing with a bully. Take deep breaths and try not to show your fear.

Stand up straight

Stand tall and look the bully in the eye. This shows that you're confident and not afraid.

Ask them to stop

Use a firm but polite tone of voice to tell the bully to stop. For example, you can say, "Please stop bothering me."

Walk away

If the bully won't stop, walk away and find a trusted adult to help you.

Find a friend

Bullies are less likely to bother you if you're with a friend. Stick together and support each other.

Tell an adult

If the bully is causing you harm or won't stop bothering you, tell a trusted adult. I would recommend both your teacher and your parents. They can help you find a solution to the problem.

Remember, it's never okay for someone to bully you, and you have the right to feel safe. If you are in this situation, tell a grown-up as soon as you can.

My family is amazing

Well, it's true! Your family is a group of people who love and care for each other no matter what. They can be your parents, siblings, grandparents, aunts, uncles, and cousins. They are the people you can always count on.

Your family is there to support you when you're happy, sad, or just need someone to talk to. They can help you learn important life skills. Your family teaches you how to communicate, problem-solve, and share with others. They also teach you values like honesty, respect, and kindness. Your family also supports you in achieving your goals and dreams. They encourage you to try new things, and they celebrate your successes with you.

Families come in all shapes and sizes! Some families have one mom or dad, while others have two moms or dads. Some families have a grandparent or other relatives living with them, while others may have just one child or many children.

There are also families with adopted children or foster children, and families that may have stepbrothers or stepsisters. Some families are made up of friends who live together and support each other like family.

No matter what type of family you have, what matters is that you love and support each other. Families can be made up of people who are related by blood or not related at all, but what's important is that they care for each other and help each other through good times and bad.

Remember, families are all unique and special in their own way.

My Mom & Dad

Our parents love us a lot! But do you sometimes find it hard to get along with your parents? It's normal to have disagreements and misunderstandings with your mom and dad from time to time. But having a good relationship with them is important for your well-being and happiness.

In this guide, we will give you some helpful tips on how to get along with your parents better. These tips will show you how to communicate effectively with your parents, how to handle conflicts calmly and respectfully, and how to show appreciation for all the things they do for you.

Soon you will be able to improve your relationship with your parents, reduce misunderstandings, and build a stronger bond with them. Remember, your parents love you and want the best for you, so it's important to work together to create a happy and harmonious home. Are you ready to learn how to get along with your parents? Let's get started!

Listen to your parents when they speak

When your parents talk to you, listen carefully and try to understand what they are saying. This shows them that you respect their opinions and care about what they have to say.

Be honest

Always tell the truth to your parents, even if it's hard. They will appreciate your honesty and it will help build trust between you.

Show gratitude

Remember to say thank you when your parents do something nice for you. They work hard to provide for you and showing gratitude lets them know you appreciate them.

Help around the house

Do your part in keeping the house clean and tidy. Offer to help with chores like washing dishes, taking out the trash, or vacuuming the floors.

Communicate calmly

When you disagree with your parents, try to communicate calmly and respectfully. Avoid yelling or using hurtful words.

Spend time together

Spend time having fun with your parents. Go for a walk, play a game, or watch a movie together.

Respect their rules

Your parents set rules to keep you safe and healthy. Follow their rules and if you disagree, try to have a calm discussion about it.

Show love and kindness

Give hugs, say "I love you" and show affection to your parents.

Remember, your parents love you and want the best for you. If you try out these ideas, you can build a strong and healthy relationship with them.

My sisters & brothers

Do you have siblings? Siblings are brothers and sisters in the same family. Sometimes, it can be hard to get along with them, but it's important to remember that they are your family and you'll be spending a lot of time with them. Remember, even if you fight with your siblings sometimes, they will always be there for you. So, are you ready to learn how to get along with your brothers and sisters? Let's get started!

Share toys and belongings

Sharing is caring! If your brother or sister wants to borrow your toy or game, let them play with it for a while.

Play together

Playing together is a great way to bond with your siblings. Find a game that you both enjoy and play it together.

Help each other

If your sibling needs help with something, like homework or chores, offer to lend a hand. They will appreciate it and may return the favor someday.

Respect each other's space

Sometimes, you and your sibling might want to do your own thing. Respect their space and let them have some alone time.

Avoid teasing or name-calling

It's important to be kind and respectful to your siblings. Avoid teasing or calling them mean names, even if you're upset with them.

Talk things out

If you have a disagreement with your sibling, try to talk it out calmly and figure out a way that works for both of you.

Show love and appreciation

Let your siblings know that you love and appreciate them. A simple hug or compliment can go a long way in strengthening your bond.

My grandparents

Do you love spending time with your grandparents? Grandparents are special people who have so much wisdom and love to share. I've got some fun ideas to help you make the most out of your time together. Whether you see them every day or just once in a while, these tips will help you build a strong and loving relationship with your grandparents. So, are you ready to learn how to have fun with your grandma and grandpa? Let's get started!

Spend time with them

Spend quality time with your grandparents by doing things you both enjoy, like playing games, reading books, or baking cookies.

Listen to their stories

Your grandparents have lots of interesting stories to share. Listen to them and ask questions. You might learn some cool stuff about your family history!

Show respect

Always be respectful to your grandparents, just like you would with any other adult. Use "please" and "thank you" and be polite.

Offer to help

Your grandparents might need some help with things like carrying groceries or setting the table. Offer to help out and they will appreciate it.

Be patient

Sometimes your grandparents might move a little slower or not understand things as quickly as you do. Be patient and try to explain things in a kind way.

Show your love

Let your grandparents know how much you love and care for them. You could make them a card or give them a hug.

Stay in touch

Even if you can't see your grandparents in person all the time, you can stay in touch by calling or video chatting with them. They will be happy to hear from you and know that you are thinking of them.

My aunts & uncles

Do you have cool aunts and uncles who love to play with you, give you presents, and take you on fun adventures? Having aunts and uncles can be awesome! I'm going to share some simple tips on how to have fun with your aunts and uncles! You'll be able to have more fun with them, share cool stories, and learn new things from them! So, are you ready to be the best niece or nephew you can be? Let's get started!

Show interest

Ask them about their hobbies, favorite foods, and things they like to do. Ask them to teach you their hobbies! This is a lovely way to spend time together.

Respect them

Always speak politely and use good manners when you are with them.

Spend time together

Plan fun activities to do together, like playing games or going to the park.

Be helpful

Offer to help them with tasks like carrying groceries or setting the table.

Share your experiences

Tell them about things you have done or learned, they may enjoy hearing your stories.

Be patient

Sometimes, they may have different ideas or opinions than you do, and it's important to listen to their perspective.

Show appreciation

Thank them for spending time with you and for the things they do for you.

Getting along with your aunts and uncles can be a lot of fun! Remember, they love you and want to spend time with you. By following these simple tips, you have lots of fun together!

Taking care of your family pet

Being lucky enough to have a cat or dog in your family is an amazing experience! Of course they are super cute and cuddly, but they can also bring lots of happiness to your life.

One of the amazing things about owning a cat or dog is the love and friendship they offer. They can be your best friend and always be there for you when you need them. They can also help you learn about responsibility by teaching you how to take care of them, like feeding them and cleaning up after them.

Cats and dogs can also help you stay active by playing with them or taking them for walks. They can even help reduce stress and anxiety just by being around you and providing a comforting presence. We love our furry friends and so here are some tips to help you to take care of them and keep them happy and healthy.

I love my cat

If you have a cat at home, it's important to take good care of them. And you can help your family make sure your cat is happy and healthy! Here are some ways you can help your family take care of your cat:

Remind your family to provide fresh water

Make sure your cat has a clean bowl of fresh water every day. Cats need water to stay healthy and hydrated.

Help with feeding

If your family is busy, you can help by feeding your cat. Ask your parents to show you how much food your cat needs and when to give it to them.

Offer to scoop the litter box

Cats need a clean litter box to go to the bathroom. Offer to scoop out the litter box every day and ask your parents to clean it out regularly.

Play with your cat

Cats need exercise and playtime. Spend some time each day playing with your cat to keep them happy and healthy.

Keep the cat's space clean

Cats need a clean and comfortable space to sleep and relax. Offer to help keep their bed and favorite spots clean.

Watch for signs of illness

Cats can get sick just like people. Watch for signs of illness like coughing, sneezing, or changes in behavior and let your family know.

Help with vet visits

Cats need to go to the vet for check-ups and shots. Offer to go with your family and help keep your cat calm during the visit.

Love and cuddle your cat

Cats need love and attention. Spend some time each day petting and cuddling your cat to show them how much you care.

Taking care of your cat can be a big responsibility, but with the help of these tips, you can make sure your cat is always happy and healthy. Your cat will be so grateful for all the love and care you give them!

I love my dog

Do you have a dog at home that you love very much? We have to make sure they are happy and healthy, and you can help your family with that! Here are some tips that are easy to understand and follow, so you can help take care of your dog. With these ideas, you can learn how to take care of your pet and make sure your furry friend is happy and healthy.

Provide fresh water

Make sure your dog has a clean bowl of fresh water every day. Every dog needs water to stay healthy and to not be thirsty.

Feed your dog

Give your dog food that is designed for their age and size. Ask your parents to help you choose the right kind of dog food.

Exercise your dog

Dogs need exercise to stay healthy and happy. Take your dog for a walk or play with them outside every day.

Keep your dog clean

Give your dog a bath when they need it, and brush their fur regularly to keep it shiny and healthy.

Train your dog

Teach your dog basic commands like sit, stay, and come. This will help keep them safe and well-behaved.

Watch for signs of illness

Dogs can get sick just like people. Watch for signs of illness like coughing, sneezing, or changes in behavior and let your family know.

Help with vet visits

It is important for dogs to go to the vet for check-ups and shots. Offer to go with your family and help keep your dog calm during the visit.

Show your dog lots of love

Dogs need love and attention. Spend some time each day playing with your dog and showing them how much you care.

Remember, taking care of your dog is an important responsibility, but it can also be a lot of fun! With these ideas you can help your family keep your furry friend healthy, happy, and loved. Always be gentle and kind to your dog, and never hesitate to ask for help from an adult if you need it. I know that you and your family can provide a wonderful life for your furry best friend.

Fun and easy exercises for kids

Exercise is really important for all kids because it helps keep your body healthy and strong. When you exercise, your heart and lungs get stronger and your muscles get stronger too. Exercise also helps your body use up extra energy, so you feel more relaxed and less stressed!

It's also good for your brain because it helps you focus better in school and be more alert. Exercise can be fun too! You can run, jump, play sports, or do other activities that get your body moving. So, make sure to get plenty of exercise every day to help keep your body and mind healthy and strong!

There are many fun exercises that young kids can do to stay active and healthy. Here are some ideas:

1. Go for a walk around your neighborhood with an adult
2. Run or play tag with your friends
3. Jump rope or hula hoop
4. Dance to your favorite songs
5. Ride your bike or scooter
6. Play basketball or soccer
7. Do simple exercises like jumping jacks, push-ups, and sit-ups
8. Swim at a pool or beach
9. Play on a playground or jungle gym
10. Try yoga or stretching exercises

Remember, it's important to find activities that you enjoy, so you'll want to keep doing them. You can also try new things and see what you like best. The most important thing is to stay active and have fun!

Cooking in the kitchen

It's important for all kids to eat healthy food because it helps your body grow and stay strong. When you eat healthy food, your body gets the vitamins and nutrients it needs to work properly. This means you will have more energy to play and learn, and you'll be less likely to get sick. Eating healthy food can also help you feel better and improve your mood.

Healthy foods include fruits, vegetables, whole grains, and lean proteins like chicken and fish. Try to avoid eating too much junk food like candy and chips, because they don't give your body the nutrition it needs.

Remember, eating healthy doesn't mean you can't enjoy your favorite foods. You can still have treats sometimes, but it's important to eat them in moderation. So, make sure to eat lots of healthy foods to help keep your body strong and healthy!

Simple meals for kids

It's important to learn how to cook simple meals because it's a great skill to have for when you grow up and become more independent. Knowing how to cook means you can make your own food and not have to rely on others to make it for you.

Cooking can also be a fun way to learn about different foods and flavors, and to experiment with making new recipes. When you cook, you get to be creative and try different combinations of ingredients to make something tasty.

Cooking can also be a great way to spend time with family and friends. You can cook together and enjoy your meals together, which can be a fun and bonding experience.

Lastly, cooking simple meals can help you make healthier food choices. When you start cooking meals for yourself, you can control what ingredients go into your food, and make sure you're eating a balanced and nutritious diet. So, learning how to cook simple meals is not only fun, but it's also an important life skill that can benefit you in many ways.

Here are some simple and easy-to-make meal ideas for kids:

Yogurt parfait with fruit and granola:

Ingredients:

- Yogurt (any flavor you like)
- Fresh fruit like bananas, strawberries and, blueberries
- Granola

Instructions:

- Start by adding a spoonful of yogurt to the bottom of a glass or bowl.
- Cut up some fresh fruit and add a layer on top of the yogurt.
- Sprinkle some granola over the fruit layer.
- Repeat these layers until you fill the glass or bowl to the top.

- Enjoy your delicious and healthy yogurt parfait!

This is a delicious and simple way to enjoy a healthy and tasty snack or breakfast. You can also try out different flavors of yogurt and fruit to find your favorite combination!

Salad with grilled chicken, veggies, and croutons

Ingredients:

- Grilled chicken breast (you can use leftover chicken if you have some)
- Lettuce (any type you like)
- Veggies (such as cherry tomatoes, cucumbers, and bell peppers)
- Croutons
- Salad dressing (any flavor you like)

Instructions:

- Wash and chop the lettuce and veggies and add them to a large bowl.
- Slice the grilled chicken breast into strips and add them to the bowl.
- Sprinkle some croutons on top of the salad.

- Add your favorite salad dressing to the bowl and toss everything together.
- Serve and enjoy your delicious and healthy salad!

This is a simple and tasty way to enjoy a healthy and filling meal. You can also add other toppings like cheese or bacon bits to make it even more flavorful!

Tuna or chicken salad with crackers and veggies:

Ingredients:

- 1 can of tuna or chicken
- 1/4 cup of mayonnaise
- 1 stalk of celery, chopped
- 1 tablespoon of diced onion (optional)
- Salt and pepper to taste
- Crackers
- Carrots and cucumbers for dipping

Instructions:

- Drain the tuna or chicken and add it to a bowl.
- Add the mayonnaise, celery, and onion to the bowl and mix well.
- Add salt and pepper to taste.
- Serve the tuna or chicken salad with crackers for scooping and dipping.

- Serve the carrots and cucumbers on the side for a healthy snack.

This is a simple and tasty way to enjoy a healthy and filling snack or light meal.

Fruit Salad:

- Cut up your favorite fruits into bite-sized pieces.
- Mix the fruit together in a bowl.
- Optional: add a drizzle of honey or a sprinkle of cinnamon for extra flavor.
- Serve and enjoy!

Here are some more simple meal ideas for kids:

- Cheese quesadillas with salsa and avocado
- English muffin pizza with pepperoni and cheese
- Turkey and cheese roll-ups with grapes
- Ham and cheese omelet with toast
- Grilled cheese sandwich with tomato soup
- Baked chicken tenders with sweet potato fries
- Pasta with marinara sauce and meatballs
- Smoothie bowl with yogurt, fruit, and granola
- Baked potato with cheese and broccoli

- Peanut butter and jelly sandwich with fruit
- Breakfast sandwich with egg, cheese, and bacon.

Remember, always ask an adult for help when using the oven or stove. Cooking can be fun and a great way to learn new skills, while also providing you with yummy and healthy meals!

Food shopping

Here are some handy ideas to help you when you go food shopping:

Make a list

Before you go to the store, write down all the things you need to buy. This will help you remember what you need and keep you from forgetting anything important.

Check the prices

Look at the prices of different foods and compare them. Sometimes the store brand can be just as good as the name brand, but cost less.

Look for healthy options

Choose foods that are good for you, like fruits, vegetables, and whole grains. Try to avoid junk food and sugary drinks.

Search for fresh vegetables

Look for vegetables that are bright in color and free from bruises or blemishes. Check if the vegetables are firm and not too soft or squishy. Smell the vegetables to make sure they don't have any bad odor. Choose vegetables that are in season as they will be fresher and taste better. Ask an adult to help you if you're not sure what to look for or need help carrying your purchases.

Read labels

Look at the labels on food packages to see what's inside. Check for things like sugar, salt, and fat content.

Ask for help

If you're not sure where to find something, ask a store employee for help. They're there to assist you.

Bring reusable bags

Bring your own bags from home to carry your groceries. This helps reduce waste and is better for the environment.

Remember to always be careful when walking around the store and watch where you're going. With these tips, you'll be a pro at grocery shopping in no time!

Safety in the kitchen

There are some things in the kitchen that could hurt you, so it's important to be very careful and always have an adult with you when you are cooking. Here are some handy ideas to keep you safe.

- Wash your hands with soap and water before handling food.
- Always use oven mitts or pot holders when handling hot dishes or pans.
- Don't touch electrical appliances with wet hands. This is really dangerous! Always unplug them when you're finished using them.

- Never touch sharp or dangerous objects like knives or scissors - ask an adult to help you with it instead.
- Don't put anything other than food in your mouth, and don't taste raw meat or eggs. These can make you feel very sick.
- Clean up any spills or messes right away to avoid slips or falls.

When you are using a microwave, make sure to never put these items into it:

- Metal objects, including foil or anything with metal trim or decorations
- Plastic containers that are not microwave safe
- Paper bags, as they can catch fire
- Eggs in their shells, as they can explode
- Styrofoam containers, which can melt and release harmful chemicals

You'll also need to keep your food safe. Here are some tips to follow:

Wash your hands

Always wash your hands before you start cooking and after handling raw meat, eggs, or other foods that could have germs on them.

Keep hot foods hot and cold foods cold

When you're cooking or serving food, make sure that hot foods stay hot and cold foods stay cold. This helps prevent bacteria from growing.

Use separate cutting boards

Use one cutting board for meat and another one for vegetables and fruits. This prevents cross-contamination and keeps your food safe to eat.

Cook food to the right temperature

Use a food thermometer to make sure that meat, poultry, and fish are cooked to the right temperature. This kills any harmful bacteria that might be in the food.

Store food properly

After you're finished cooking, store leftovers in the refrigerator or freezer. Don't leave food out at room temperature for too long, as this can cause bacteria to grow.

Don't eat raw dough or batter

Raw dough or batter can contain harmful germs like E. coli and Salmonella. So, don't taste or eat them.

Don't share utensils or drinks

Sharing utensils or drinks with others can spread germs and make you sick. Use your own utensils and drinks to avoid sharing germs.

By following these safety tips in the kitchen, you can help prevent accidents and injuries while cooking and baking.

Making chores fun

Doing chores is an important part of growing up and helping out at home. Chores are tasks that you can do around the house to help keep things clean and organized. Even though they might not be the most fun thing to do, they are very important for you and your family. Let's explore some simple tips for doing chores that are easy to understand and follow. When you are doing your chores, you can play some music too and make them fun!

Putting away toys

Pick up all the toys and put them back in their proper place. If you have a toy box, make sure to place them in the box neatly.

Sweeping

Grab a broom and sweep up any crumbs or dirt on the floor. Make sure to sweep everything into a dustpan and throw it away in the trash.

Watering plants

Fill a watering can with water and gently pour it over the soil around the plant. Be careful not to overwater or spill water on the floor.

Setting the table

Get out the plates, cups, utensils, and napkins and place them in their proper spots on the table. Don't forget to put out any condiments or drinks.

Folding laundry

Take a pile of clean clothes and fold them neatly into piles. Put each pile away in the proper drawers or closet.

Dusting

Use a cloth or duster to wipe down surfaces like tables, shelves, and picture frames. Make sure to get in all the corners and hard-to-reach places.

Great job learning about some simple chores you can do to help around the house! Remember, doing chores is an important way to be responsible and help your family. By following these steps, you can do your part and make a big difference in keeping your home clean and organized.

Being kind to the environment

It's important to be kind to the environment because it's our home. We need to take care of it so we can have clean air to breathe, water to drink, and places for animals and plants to live happily. When we are kind to the environment, we're also helping ourselves and everyone around us.

Recycle

When we recycle things like paper, plastic, and cans, we help save energy and resources. This means we can make new things without hurting our planet!

Lights and electrics

Turn off lights and electronics when you're not using them. This saves energy and helps the environment.

Save water

Turning off the tap while brushing our teeth or taking shorter showers helps save water. This way, we have enough clean water for everyone, including the animals and plants.

Plastic

Plastic takes a very long time to break down, and it can hurt animals if they eat it or get tangled in it. Instead, we can use reusable bags, bottles, and containers, which we can wash and use again and again.

Plant trees

Trees are important because they give us oxygen, which we need to breathe. They also give homes to birds and other animals. So, let's plant more trees and make our environment beautiful and healthy.

Don't litter

Throwing trash on the ground can make our playground dirty and hurt animals. Always put trash in the proper bin so we can keep our world clean and safe.

Paper

When we use a lot of paper, we need to cut down more trees. Trees are important because they clean our air and give homes to many animals. Instead of using paper, we can draw on both sides of it or use electronic devices, like tablets, to read and write.

Cars and transport

Cars make smoke that can make our air dirty and harder to breathe. Instead of driving, we can walk, ride bikes, or take public transportation like buses and trains. This helps keep our air clean and our bodies healthy.

By doing these things, we can show kindness to the environment and make our planet a better place for everyone to live, play, and grow.

Gardening for kids

Let's talk about gardening! Gardening is when we plant seeds, help them grow into plants, and take care of them. It's like being a superhero for flowers, fruits, and vegetables. Gardening is important because it helps us grow delicious food and beautiful flowers. It's also great for our planet, as plants clean the air we breathe and give homes to little creatures like birds and butterflies.

Here are some cool reasons why gardening is perfect for you:

Get your hands dirty

Gardening lets you play in the dirt and learn about nature. It's a fun way to be outside and enjoy the sunshine!

Learn responsibility

Taking care of plants helps you learn how to be responsible. You'll water them, protect them from bugs, and watch them grow strong and healthy.

Healthy food

When you grow your own fruits and vegetables, you can enjoy fresh, tasty, and healthy snacks right from your garden!

Teamwork

Gardening is an awesome way to work together with your family and friends. You can learn new things, share ideas, and make your garden beautiful as a team.

So, grab your gloves, a shovel, and let's start gardening! It's a fantastic way to have fun, learn, and help our planet.

How to grow vegetables

Are you ready for a super fun and tasty adventure? Let's talk about growing vegetables at home! Growing your own vegetables is like having a tiny grocery store right in your backyard. It's a fantastic way to enjoy fresh, yummy, and healthy food.

Super fresh food

When you grow vegetables at home, you can pick them right when they're ripe and eat them straight from your garden. They'll be the freshest, most delicious veggies you've ever tasted!

Healthy snacks

Homegrown vegetables are full of vitamins and nutrients that help you grow strong and healthy. Plus, they make awesome snacks for when you're hungry or need energy to play.

Save the Earth

Growing your own vegetables means less trips to the store, which means fewer car rides and less pollution. It's a great way to help our planet stay clean and green.

Learn and have fun

Gardening is a super fun way to learn about nature, plants, and how things grow. You'll get to play in the dirt, watch your plants change, and discover new things every day.

Proud moments

When you grow your own vegetables, you can be proud of the hard work you've done. Share your harvest with your family and friends, and show them what an amazing gardener you are!

Growing vegetables at home is an awesome way to have fun, learn new things, and enjoy tasty, healthy food. Now, let's learn how you can start your very own vegetable garden!

Here are some easy vegetables to grow in countries including the UK and USA:

1. Tomatoes
2. Carrots
3. Peas
4. Lettuce
5. Radishes

Now, let's learn how to grow these tasty vegetables step by step:

Pick a spot

Find a place in your garden or yard that gets plenty of sunlight. This will help your vegetables grow big and strong.

Prepare the soil

With a grown-up's help, dig the soil to loosen it up. Add some compost or plant food to make it rich and healthy for your plants.

Choose your seeds

Pick the vegetable seeds you want to grow, like tomatoes or carrots. You can find seeds at a garden store or online.

Plant the seeds

Follow the instructions on the seed packet to know how deep and far apart to plant the seeds. With a grown-up's help, make little holes in the soil and drop the seeds in. Cover them gently with soil.

Water and care

Water your seeds regularly, and keep the soil moist but not too wet. As your plants grow, protect them from bugs and give them plenty of love!

Harvest time

When your vegetables are big and ripe, it's time to pick them! Enjoy the tasty food you've grown, and share it with your family and friends.

Growing vegetables is a fantastic way to learn about nature, have fun, and enjoy delicious food. So, put on your gardening gloves and let's get growing!

How to grow flowers

Did you know that growing flowers is really good for our planet? It's true! Flowers are like nature's little helpers. Let's learn why they're so important:

Clean air

Flowers help clean the air by taking in something called "carbon dioxide" and giving out "oxygen," which we need to breathe. So, they make our air fresher and healthier!

Homes for animals

Many animals, like bees, butterflies, and birds, need flowers to live. Flowers give them food to eat and a place to rest. By growing flowers, we're helping these little creatures have a happy home.

Save the bees

Bees are super important because they help our fruits and veggies grow. They visit flowers to collect something called "pollen." When bees move from flower to flower, they help create new plants! Growing flowers means more yummy food for everyone.

Happy Earth

Flowers make the planet more colorful and beautiful. When we have lots of flowers, it makes our world a happier place for people, animals, and even the Earth itself.
By growing flowers, we're helping our planet be a better, healthier, and happier home for all of us. So, put on your gardening gloves and let's start planting!

Here are some easy flowers to grow in countries like the UK and USA:

1. Sunflowers

2. Marigolds
3. Pansies
4. Tulips
5. Daffodils
6. Native wildflowers

Now, let's learn how to grow these lovely flowers step by step:

Pick a spot

Find a place in your garden or yard that gets lots of sunlight. Flowers love sunshine, and it helps them grow big and colorful.

Prepare the soil

With a grown-up's help, dig the soil to loosen it up. Add some compost or plant food to make it rich and healthy for your flowers.

Choose your seeds

Pick the flower seeds you want to grow, like sunflowers or marigolds. You can find seeds at a garden store or online.

Plant the seeds

Follow the instructions on the seed packet to know how deep and far apart to plant the seeds. With a grown-up's help, make little holes in the soil and drop the seeds in. Cover them gently with soil.

Water and care

Water your seeds regularly, and keep the soil moist but not too wet. As your flowers grow, protect them from bugs and give them lots of love!

Watch them bloom

Be patient and watch as your flowers grow and bloom into beautiful colors. Enjoy their beauty and share it with your family and friends.

Growing flowers is a fun way to learn about nature and make your world more beautiful. So, grab your gardening gloves and let's start planting!

Looking fabulous and smelling great

Washing your teeth

Washing and brushing your teeth is super important to keep your teeth healthy and your smile bright. Let's learn why it's important, how often to do it, and how to do it:

Brushing your teeth helps remove leftover food and yucky stuff called "plaque" that can cause cavities or make your breath smell bad. Washing your teeth keeps your mouth clean and your smile shiny! You should brush your teeth at least two times every day: once in the morning when you wake up, and once before bedtime.

Here's a simple guide to brushing your teeth:

- Get a toothbrush and some toothpaste. Use a small, pea-sized amount of toothpaste on your toothbrush.
- Hold your toothbrush at a slight angle against your teeth and gently move it back and forth in small circles. Make sure to brush every tooth, even the ones in the back!
- Don't forget to brush the front, back, and top of each tooth. Gently brush your tongue, too, to keep your breath fresh.
- When you're done, spit out the toothpaste into the sink and rinse your mouth with water. Don't swallow the toothpaste!
- Rinse your toothbrush and put it away in a clean, dry place.

By brushing your teeth every day, you'll have a clean and healthy mouth, and your smile will be bright and beautiful. So, don't forget to wash your teeth, and show off your sparkling smile!

Using the shower and bath

It's important to have a shower or bath regularly because it helps to keep our bodies clean and healthy. When we go outside or do activities, we can get dirty, and washing ourselves helps to remove dirt, sweat, and germs from our skin. This helps to prevent us from getting sick or having skin problems. Additionally, having a bath or shower can help us relax and feel refreshed after a long day.

Using the bathroom

Bathroom etiquette is about following rules to keep the bathroom clean and safe for everyone to use. Here are some simple tips:

- Always flush the toilet after using it.
- Wash your hands with soap and water after using the toilet or touching any surfaces in the bathroom.
- Throw used toilet paper in the toilet and not on the floor.
- Don't waste water by leaving the tap running unnecessarily.

- Always close the toilet lid after flushing to prevent germs from spreading.
- Don't take too long in the bathroom, especially when others are waiting to use it.

Being nice in the bathroom is a way to show you care about others. It means using the bathroom the right way, making sure it's clean when you're done, and remembering that people like their privacy.

When you're feeling ill

When you need to cough or sneeze, it's important to be polite and think about others. Here's how to do it in a nice way:

Cover your mouth and nose

When you feel a cough or sneeze coming, cover your mouth and nose with the inside of your elbow or with a tissue. This helps keep germs from spreading to other people.

Turn away

If you're near someone, try to turn your head away from them when you cough or sneeze. This helps keep the germs from going towards them.

Use a tissue

If you have a tissue handy, use it to cover your mouth and nose when you cough or sneeze. Then, throw it away in a bin right away.

Wash your hands

After coughing or sneezing, make sure to wash your hands with soap and water or use hand sanitizer to get rid of germs.

By being polite when you cough or sneeze, you're helping to keep others healthy and showing them that you care about their well-being.

How to take care of your clothes

Taking care of your clothes and keeping them clean is important for a few reasons. Clean clothes help you smell fresh and nice. When we play, run, or do activities, our clothes can get dirty and smelly. Washing them makes them smell good again!

When your clothes are clean and tidy, you look neat and well-groomed. This helps you make a good impression on your friends, teachers, and grown-ups. Taking care of your clothes teaches you how to be responsible and look after the things you own. This is a great skill to have as you grow up. Plus when you take good care of your clothes, they last longer and stay in better condition. This means you can enjoy wearing them for a long time! Here are some simple things you can do to take care of your clothes:

Keep your clothes safe

When you are finished with wearing your clothes, put them in a basket instead of leaving them on the floor of your bedroom or bathroom.

Sort your clothes

Sort your clothes by color and fabric before washing them. This will prevent colors from bleeding and clothes from getting damaged.

Wash your clothes

Follow the care labels on your clothes to know how to wash them. Use the right temperature and the right amount of detergent. Don't overload the washing machine.

Dry your clothes

Follow the care labels on your clothes to know how to dry them. Some clothes can be tumble-dried, while others need to be air-dried. Hang your clothes properly to avoid stretching or wrinkling.

Iron your clothes

Iron your clothes to keep them looking neat and clean. Follow the care labels on your clothes to know the right temperature for ironing. Make sure you get help from your parents when you're doing this as the iron can be very hot.

Store your clothes

Store your clothes in a clean and dry place. Fold them neatly or hang them on hangers to avoid creases and wrinkles. Don't leave them on the floor! Remember to always ask an adult for help if you are unsure of what to do!

Superhero self-care habits

Self-care is important because it means taking care of yourself so that you can feel good both physically and emotionally. When you take care of yourself, you are giving yourself love and attention, just like you do with your friends and family. This can help you feel happier, healthier, and more confident. It's important to remember that taking care of yourself is not selfish, it's necessary for a happy and healthy life.

Get enough sleep

Getting enough sleep is essential for staying healthy and feeling good. Aim to get at least 8-10 hours of sleep each night.

Eat healthy foods

Eating a balanced diet that includes lots of fruits and vegetables is important for keeping your body strong and healthy.

Exercise regularly

Regular exercise, like playing outside or participating in sports, helps keep your body strong and healthy. Try to get at least 60 minutes of exercise each day.

Take breaks and relax

Taking breaks to relax and do things you enjoy, like reading a book or playing a game, can help you feel less stressed and more refreshed.

Practice good hygiene

Taking care of your body, like washing your hands and brushing your teeth, is important for staying healthy and feeling good about yourself.

Sunscreen

Wear sunscreen every day, to protect your skin from harmful rays from the sun.

Taking care of ourselves is very important, especially for young kids. By practicing self-care, we can stay healthy, happy, and feel good about ourselves. Remember to take breaks, get enough rest, exercise, eat healthy, and take care of our hygiene. These habits can help us feel good both physically and mentally, which is very important for our overall well-being.

Communication tips for kids

Communication is an important skill that helps us express ourselves and understand others. Whether we are talking to our family, friends, or classmates, it's essential to communicate effectively. I will go through eight simple communication tips that will be really useful to help you boost your communication skills and build happy relationships with your friends, family and everyone you meet.

Listen carefully

When someone is speaking, give them your full attention and focus on what they are saying.

Speak clearly

Make sure to speak clearly and slowly so that others can understand you.

Use polite words

Always use words like "please" and "thank you" when you are talking to others.

Be honest

Always tell the truth, even if it's hard.

Stay calm

If you feel upset or angry, take a deep breath and try to stay calm.

Respect others

Treat others the way you want to be treated.

Ask questions

If you don't understand something, ask questions to make sure you do.

Use your body language

Sometimes our body language can communicate how we feel better than words, so pay attention to your own body language and others' body language as well.

By following these communication tips, you can have better relationships with your family, friends, and classmates, and make sure that everyone feels heard and understood. Don't be afraid to speak up, listen actively, and show empathy and respect to others. With lots of practice you can become a great communicator!

Creativity and innovation

Being creative is a super fun and important part of growing up. Being creative helps you show your feelings and thoughts in your own special way. You can make art, music, or stories to share how you feel. When you're creative, you think of new ideas and solve problems. This helps your brain grow and learn better. Creative activities like drawing, painting, dancing, or singing are lots of fun! They let you enjoy yourself and have a great time. When you share your creative work with others, it can help you make new friends who like the same things as you do. Creating something unique and special makes you feel proud of yourself. It's a wonderful way to build confidence and feel good about who you are.

Being creative is a fantastic way to have fun, learn new things, make friends and feel good about yourself! Here are 8 fun and easy activities to help you be more creative. Just follow these simple steps:

DIY bookmarks

Cut a strip of thick paper or cardboard.

Decorate it with drawings, stickers, or paint.

Punch a hole at the top and tie a ribbon or string through it.

Use your new bookmark in your favorite book!

Create a comic strip

Fold a piece of paper into sections to make panels.

Draw your own characters and create a funny or exciting story.

Fill in the panels with your drawings and add speech bubbles.

Share your comic strip with friends or family.

Write a poem

Think about something that makes you happy, sad, or excited.

Write down words or phrases that describe those feelings.

Arrange your words into lines or stanzas to create a poem.

Read your poem out loud or share it with someone you know.

Make a vision board

Think about your dreams, goals, and things you like.

Cut out pictures, words, or quotes from magazines or printouts.

Arrange them on a poster board or large piece of paper.

Hang your vision board in your room to inspire you every day.

Design your own board game

Draw a game board on a large piece of paper or cardboard.

Create game pieces, cards, and rules for your game.

Invite friends or family to play your new game and have fun!

Make a scrapbook

Collect photos, ticket stubs, or other mementos from your life.

Arrange them on pages in a photo album or notebook.

Add captions, drawings, or stickers to personalize each page.

Share your scrapbook with friends or family to relive memories.

Design a T-shirt

Find a plain T-shirt or ask a grown-up for help to buy one.

Use fabric markers, paint, or iron-on transfers to create a unique design.

Wear your one-of-a-kind T-shirt or give it as a gift.

Create a treasure hunt

Write or draw clues on pieces of paper.

Hide the clues around your house or garden.

Invite friends or family to follow the clues and find a hidden "treasure" like a small toy or treat.

Try these creative activities and let your imagination run wild!

Making smart decisions

Learning to make smart decisions is an important skill to learn as you grow up. Making smart decisions helps you stay safe and avoid getting hurt. For example, choosing to wear a helmet when riding a bike can protect your head. When you make good choices, you feel proud of yourself and have a better time. For example, if you choose to finish your homework before playing, you can enjoy your free time without worrying about it. Making smart decisions helps you solve problems and find solutions. For example, if you're having trouble with schoolwork, deciding to ask for help can make things easier.

As you grow up, you'll need to make more and more choices on your own. Learning to make good decisions helps you become more responsible and independent. When you make smart decisions, you build confidence in yourself and your abilities. This helps you feel strong and capable in different situations. Making good choices also helps you be a good friend to others. For example, if you choose to share and be kind, you'll have stronger friendships.

By learning to make smart decisions, you're growing into a responsible and confident person who can handle challenges and enjoy a happy, successful life! Here are some ways you can make smart decisions.

Think about your choices

When you have to make a decision, take some time to think about the options you have. For example, if you need to pick a school project topic, write down a few ideas that you're interested in.

Ask yourself questions

Consider the possible outcomes for each choice. Ask yourself, "What could happen if I choose this?" or "How will this choice make me feel?" For example, if you're deciding whether to join a sports team or an art club, think about which one you enjoy more and how it will fit into your schedule.

Gather information

Learn more about your options by talking to others, reading, or researching. For example, if you're choosing a new book to read, ask your friends for suggestions or read book summaries online.

Consider your values

Think about what matters most to you and how your choices line up with your values. For example, if you value honesty, choose to tell the truth even when it's difficult.

Weigh the pros and cons

Make a list of the good things and not-so-good things about each choice. This can help you see which option is best for you. For example, if you're deciding whether to save your allowance or spend it, consider the benefits of saving (like buying something bigger later) versus spending it now.

Take your time

Don't rush your decision. Give yourself time to think it through. Sometimes, sleeping on it can help you make a better choice.

Talk to someone you trust

Ask a parent, teacher, or friend for advice. They might have helpful suggestions or insights to guide your decision.

Trust your instincts

Pay attention to how you feel about each choice. Your feelings can help guide you to the right decision.

Remember, making smart decisions takes practice. As you learn and grow, you'll get better at it. Keep trying, and don't be afraid to ask for help when you need it!

A kid's guide to setting goals

Learning to set goals is really important. Setting goals helps you stay focused on what you want to achieve. For example, if your goal is to learn a new sport, you'll practice and work hard to get better at it. Goals help you see how much progress you're making. When you reach a goal, you can feel proud of your hard work and see how much you've grown. Achieving goals can make you feel more confident in your abilities. This helps you believe in yourself and try new things.

Setting goals helps you plan your time and effort. For example, if you have a goal to read a certain number of books, you can plan when to read and track your progress. Working towards goals helps you develop good habits, like being responsible, patient, and persistent. These habits will help you throughout your life.

Setting and achieving goals can be fun and exciting! It's a great way to try new things and see what you're capable of.

By learning to set goals, you're taking control of your own growth and success. You'll become more confident, organized, and ready to take on new challenges!

How to set goals

Choose a goal

Think about something you want to achieve or improve. For example, you might want to read more books, learn to play an instrument, or get better at a sport.

Be specific

Make your goal clear and specific. Instead of saying "I want to read more," say "I want to read 5 books this month."

Break it down

If your goal is big, break it into smaller, manageable steps. For example, if you want to learn to play the guitar, start with learning one song at a time.

Make a plan

Create a plan for how you'll work towards your goal. If you love soccer and you want to improve your soccer skills, plan to practice for 30 minutes every day after school.

Set a deadline

Give yourself a deadline to help stay focused. For example, if you want to finish a school project, set a date to have it completed by.

Track your progress

Keep track of how you're doing. You can use a chart, journal, or app to see your progress. If your goal is to run a mile, track your running times each week.

Stay motivated

Think about why you want to achieve your goal and what it will mean to you. This can help you stay excited and motivated. For example, if you want to save money to buy a new toy, remind yourself why that toy is important to you.

Get support

Share your goal with a parent, teacher, or friend who can help and encourage you. They can also celebrate your achievements with you!

Adjust as needed

If you find your goal is too easy or too hard, adjust it to make it more realistic. For example, if you've already read 5 books in two weeks, increase your goal to 10 books for the month.

Celebrate your success

When you reach your goal, celebrate your hard work and achievement! You can give yourself a reward - like a treat or a fun activity.

Remember, setting and working towards goals takes practice. Keep trying, and you'll get better at it as you grow!

Time management for kids

Time management is important to learn! Managing your time helps you finish your tasks, like homework or chores, on time. This way, you won't have to rush or worry about not finishing them. When you plan your time well, you'll feel less stressed because you know what you need to do and when to do it. Good time management means you can finish your work faster, leaving more time for fun activities like playing with friends, sports, or hobbies.

Learning to manage your time at a young age helps you develop good habits, like being responsible and organized. These habits will help you in school and later in life. Time management also helps you find a balance between school, activities, and family time. This way, you can enjoy all the things you love without feeling overwhelmed.

By learning time management, you're setting yourself up for success and making your days more enjoyable and less stressful. Here are some tips to help you manage your time.

Make a schedule

Create a daily or weekly schedule to plan your time. Write down your activities, like school, homework, and playtime. For example, you can set aside 4:00-5:00 pm for homework and 5:00-6:00 pm for playing outside.

Prioritize tasks

Put the most important tasks first. For example, finish your homework before watching TV or playing video games.

Break big tasks into smaller steps: If you have a big task, like a school project, break it into smaller steps. For example, first research your topic, then make an outline, and finally, write your report.

Set deadlines

Give yourself deadlines for tasks to help you stay on track. For example, if you need to finish a book report in a week, set a deadline to finish reading the book in three days.

Use a timer

Set a timer when working on tasks to help you stay focused. You could set a timer for 20 minutes of focused homework time, followed by a 5-minute break.

Avoid distractions

Find a quiet place to work and put away distractions like your phone or toys. This will help you concentrate on your tasks.

Ask for help

If you're having trouble managing your time or finishing tasks, ask a parent or teacher for help. They can give you advice and support.

Be flexible

Sometimes things don't go as planned, and that's okay. Adjust your schedule as needed, and remember to give yourself some extra time for unexpected events.

Learn to say no

If you're too busy or have too much on your plate, it's okay to say no to new activities or commitments.

Reward yourself

When you finish a task or manage your time well, reward yourself with a small treat or fun activity.

By following these tips, you'll be able to manage your time better and enjoy a more balanced and stress-free life. Keep practicing, and you'll get better at time management as you grow!

Simple strategies for overcoming challenges

No matter what age you are, we all have challenges we need to overcome every day!

Learning to overcome challenges is really important for a few reasons.

Overcoming challenges helps you build resilience, which means you're able to bounce back from difficult situations. When you face challenges, you need to find solutions. This helps you develop problem-solving skills that you can use in all areas of your life.

Challenges can sometimes result in mistakes, but that's okay! Learning from your mistakes is a really important part of growing and improving. When you overcome challenges, you feel proud of yourself and more confident in your abilities.

Overcoming challenges can help you achieve your goals, whether it's learning a new skill or finishing a project. Facing challenges can be fun and exciting! It's a great way to try new things and see what you're capable of.By learning to overcome challenges, you're growing into a strong and capable person who can handle anything that comes your way!

To help you overcome challenges, here are some useful ideas.

Stay positive

Focus on what you can do, not what you can't. For example, if you're struggling with a math problem, tell yourself "I can figure this out!"

Break it down

If a challenge seems too big, break it into smaller, more manageable steps. For example, if you have a big project due, break it into smaller tasks like researching, outlining, and writing.

Get help

Ask a parent, teacher, or friend for help. They can offer advice or support. For example, if you're having trouble with a science experiment, ask your teacher for help.

Keep trying

Don't give up if you don't succeed at first. Keep trying and learn from your mistakes. For example, if you're learning a new skill like juggling, keep practicing even if you drop the balls at first.

Be flexible

Sometimes things don't go as planned, and that's okay. Be flexible, think about it and see what you can change. For example, if a project takes longer than expected, adjust your schedule and prioritize your time.

Stay calm

Take deep breaths and stay calm when faced with a challenge. This can help you think more clearly and make better decisions.

Celebrate small victories

Celebrate each step you take towards overcoming a challenge. This can motivate you to keep going. For example, if you finish a chapter in a challenging book, reward yourself with a small treat.

Remember, facing and overcoming challenges takes practice. Keep trying, and you'll become more confident and capable as you grow!

First aid for kids: What to do in an emergency

Learning first aid is really useful for all kids. Knowing first aid can help you be prepared to help someone in an emergency situation. This can help save someone's life or prevent further harm.
Learning first aid also helps you know how to take care of yourself in an emergency situation.

Knowing first aid can also give you the confidence to handle an emergency situation calmly and effectively. It also teaches you about responsibility and taking care of others. It helps you become a more responsible and caring person.

First aid skills can also be used in everyday situations, like treating a cut or scrape. Knowing how to take care of minor injuries can help prevent infections and other complications. Learning first aid can also lead to future opportunities in healthcare or other service-related fields when you're older too!.

By learning first aid, you're becoming a more responsible and caring person who can help others in an emergency. It's an important skill that you can use throughout your life.

Here are some first aid tips that you can use in emergency situations, with examples:

Call for help

If someone is hurt, call for an adult or emergency services right away. Make sure to give them your location and what happened.

Stay calm

Stay calm and reassure the person who is hurt. This can help them feel more relaxed and less scared.

Assess the situation

Look for any immediate dangers, like fire or falling objects. Move the person to a safe location if necessary.

Stop bleeding

If someone is bleeding, use a clean cloth or bandage to apply pressure to the wound, until help arrives.

Treat burns

Run cool water over a burn for at least 10 minutes to cool the area. Cover the area that has the burn with a clean, dry cloth.

Treat cuts and scrapes

Clean cuts and scrapes with water, then cover with a bandage or gauze.

Remember, first aid is important but it's always best to get help from an adult or emergency services if you're not sure what to do. Keep practicing and learning, and you'll become more confident and capable in helping others in emergency situations.

Click smart: Staying safe online

Many of us use the internet! Whether it's watching videos, looking at websites, playing with apps or messaging our friends, there is a whole world of people and information available when we connect online. Some of it can help us stay in touch with our friends and learn new things. But some of it can really be bad for us - sometimes people can get bullied online, or strangers can get in contact with us and this can lead to trouble.

Digital habits mean how you use technology, like how much time you spend on it, what you do, and how you talk to others. It's important to learn how to use social media and technology the right way. This means being careful about things like bullies, scams, and things that are not for kids. By doing this, you can use technology in a good way and keep yourself safe.

Here are some handy tips for kids to stay safe online

When you're online, it's important to keep your personal information - which means your name, your date of birth, your address and phone number, completely private. This helps prevent identity theft or cyberbullying. Never share any personal info about yourself online.

There are many scams online, like fake websites or emails that can trick you into giving away your personal information or money. Knowing how to recognize these scams helps you avoid them. If you're not sure about something online, check with a parent or teacher before you click on a link or download something.

Cyberbullying can happen online through social media or messaging apps. Sometimes we can feel like we are in trouble, but we don't want to tell our parents. No matter what problems you have in your life, you can always find an adult to talk to. This can be a parent, a teacher, a grandparent or an aunt or uncle.

There are some things online that are not appropriate for kids to see, like violent or adult content.

When you post things online, it can affect what people think of you. This can happen now, or even in the future. If you post a picture of you today, people might still be able to see it in 20 or 30 years time! So never share private or family pictures online. This means being responsible and thinking before you post!

It's really important to be safe while you are online. If you feel nervous, worried or anxious at any time, turn off the internet (or maybe get rid of it altogether) and have some fun with your friends in real life. It's really important to balance the time you spend online with other activities, like playing outside, doing homework, or spending time with family and friends.

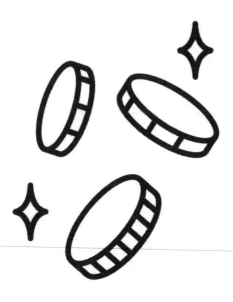

Cash rules: Money smarts for kids

How to earn and manage your pocket money

Pocket money is a small amount of money that your parents or guardians give you to spend on things you like. It's a way for you to learn how to manage money and make choices about what you want to buy. It can be earned by doing chores around the house, or it can be given as a regular allowance. It's important to learn how to use your pocket money wisely, so you can save for things you really want or need. By understanding how to use pocket money, you can learn important skills for managing your money in the future.

Here are some fun ways you can earn pocket money:

Doing chores

You can earn money by doing household chores like cleaning your room, washing dishes, setting the table every morning or helping with the laundry.

Babysitting

If you're responsible and good with kids, you can offer to babysit for families in your neighborhood.

Selling items

You can sell items you no longer need, like old toys or clothes, at a garage sale or a yard sale at your house.

Dog walking

Offer to walk your dog every day to earn some pocket money.

Helping with yard work

You can offer to help with yard work like raking leaves, mowing the lawn, or watering plants. By earning pocket money, you can learn about responsibility and the value of hard work, and earn some money you can spend on things you love!

How to save and budget your pocket money

Wish you could make your pocket money go further and last longer? Well here are some useful tips on how to save and budget your pocket money!

Set a goal

Decide what you want to save for, like a new toy or game. Set a savings goal and try to save a little bit each week or month.

Make a budget

Plan how you will spend your pocket money. Decide what you want to buy and make a list of them and how much they cost. Then, decide how much you can spend on each item.

Wait for sales

Look for sales or discounts on things you want to buy. This can help you save money and get more for your pocket money.

Avoid impulse buys

Think carefully before you buy something. Ask yourself if you really need it, or if you just want it because it looks cool.

Keep track of your spending

Write down what you spend your pocket money on. This can help you see where your money is going and make adjustments if needed.

By learning how to save and budget your pocket money, you can make your money go further and save up for the things you really want. It's an important skill that you can use throughout your life.

Businesses that kids can start today

Have you ever had a dream of starting your own business at home? Starting your own business can be a great idea for many reasons! Starting your own business lets you use your creativity and imagination to create something unique. It's such an amazing feeling to turn your ideas into a real life business!

Starting your own business can help you earn money and learn about managing finances. You'll be able to save your profit to buy things you really like, even buy a delicious dinner for your family, gifts for your friends or new toys for your pet!

Starting a business can teach you new skills like marketing, sales, and budgeting. Running your own business gives you independence and the freedom to make your own choices. Having your own business is a very cool thing to do! You are your own boss and you get to make all the decisions (with your parents help of course!)

Starting a business can help you build confidence and self-esteem. Having a fun business can really help to make you feel happy and excited about everything in your life! When you start your own business and see it grow, you can feel proud of your accomplishments.

By starting your own business, you can learn many valuable skills that will benefit you throughout your life. It's also a great way to have fun and do something you enjoy while making money. So here are some creative business ideas that you can start from home:

Jewelry making

You can make necklaces, bracelets, or earrings using beads, string, or wire. You can sell your jewelry online or at local markets.

Art prints

You can create your own artwork or illustrations, and then turn them into prints that people can buy. You can sell your prints on online marketplaces or on your own website.

T-shirt design

You can design your own t-shirts using fabric markers, paint, or iron-on transfers. You can sell your t-shirts online or at local markets.

Greeting cards

You can design and create your own greeting cards using cardstock, stickers, and other craft supplies. You can sell your cards online or at local stores.

Baked goods

You can make your own baked goods, like cookies, cupcakes, or brownies, and sell them to friends and family or at local markets.

Pet treats

If you love animals, you can make your own pet treats using simple ingredients like peanut butter, carrots, and oats. You can sell your treats to pet owners in your community.

Customized phone cases

You can decorate phone cases with paint, stickers, or markers, and sell them online or at local markets.

Hair accessories

You can make your own hair accessories, like headbands or bows, using fabric or ribbon. You can sell your accessories online or at local markets.

By starting your own creative business, you can learn valuable skills like entrepreneurship, marketing, and budgeting. It's a great way to earn money doing something you love and share your creativity with others.

You've done it!

Congratulations, young superhero! You have completed your training in essential life skills and are now ready to take on the world! Remember, life is full of surprises, but with the skills you've learned in this book, you have the power to overcome any challenge that comes your way.

Always remember to communicate clearly, think carefully and make informed decisions. Don't be afraid to take risks and try new things, because that's how you grow and learn. And most importantly, believe in yourself and your abilities, because you have the potential to achieve anything you set your mind to.

Now go out there and show the world what you're made of! You are unstoppable, you are a superhero, and you have the power to make a difference. Keep learning, keep growing, and keep shining bright like the star you are! Good luck, young superhero!

Before you go, I have a small request to make. I would really appreciate it if you could review this book and share your lessons learned. Doing so will help me a lot in getting this book out to other kids who can benefit from the tips and strategies I have shared.

Made in United States
Orlando, FL
30 March 2023

31574952R00076